101 EFFECTIVE WAYS OF MENTORING TEENS IN THE 21ST CENTURY

FELICITY W. GITHINJI, GERALD G. GITHINJI AND MARY W. MUHIA

Felicity et al.,

Copyright © 2019 Felicity W. Githinji, Gerald G. Githinji and Mary W. Muhia Author Name

ISBN: 978-9966-135-68-1

DEDICATION

This book is dedicated to all teens wishing them a successful transition to adulthood as they aspire to Mentor others in life

Felicity et al.,

ACKNOWLEDGMENTS

We would like to acknowledge everyone who took their time to
read and correct this book from start to finish.

AUTHORS WORDS

A mentor is a person or friend who guides a less experienced person by building trust and modeling positive behaviors. It is someone willing to spend his or her time and expertise to guide the development of another person. Parents, teachers and society should devote their time to actively enrich their children, ensuring that the child's individual needs are addressed and that the children are able to reach their full potential.

Train Your Teen/Give Education

Knowledge to Apply

Train a child how to live the right way. Then even when he is old, he will still live that way.

Proverbs 22:6

Reference

2

Create a Conducive and Free Environment

Knowledge to Apply

Parents, do not treat your children in such a way as to make them angry. Instead, raise them with Christian discipline and instruction.

Ephesians 6:4

Reference

3

Watch What You Say to Your Teen

Knowledge to Apply

What you say can preserve life or destroy it; so you must accept the consequences of your words. Proverbs 18:21

Reference

4

Give Your Teen Attention

Knowledge to Apply

Teens are starving for attention from an adult who believes in them. A teen that does not have a healthy relationship with an adult often lacks confidence.

Reference

Conner, J. (2017). 10 Tips to Mentor Youth like a Superstar. Retrieved from https://drjulieconnor.com/10-mentoring-tips/

5

Introduce Your Teen to Things You Like to Do

Knowledge to Apply

This is a useful way for your teen to learn more about you and understand you better.

Reference

Grace Point (2017). Mentoring. Retrieved from https://www.gracepointwellness.org/82-parenting/article/4732-mentoring

6

Discipline Your Teen

Knowledge to Apply

Discipline them but let them see their mistake first

Whoever spares the rod hates their children, but the one who loves their children is careful to discipline them. Proverbs 13:24

Discipline your son, for in that there is hope; do not be a willing party to his death" (Prov. 19:18).

Reference

Holy Bible, New International Version®, NIV® Copyright ©1973, 1978, 1984, 2011 by Biblica, Inc.®

7

Treat All Your Teens Equally

Knowledge to Apply

Favoritism (even perceived favoritism) fosters bitterness and resentment in the hearts of the teens who feel they have been slighted.

Reference

Munroe, M., & Burrows, D. (2007). *Kingdom Parenting*. Destiny Image Publishers.

8

Provide For Your Teens

Knowledge to Apply

As a parent it is your responsibility to provide for your teens the basic needs: food, shelter and clothing. Where possible also, supply for their other personal needs in limitations.

Reference

Aviles, A., & Helfrich, C. (2004). Life skill service needs: Perspectives of homeless youth. Journal of Youth and Adolescence, 33(4), 331-338.

9

Be a Positive Role Model

Knowledge to Apply

Do the things you would want you teen to emulate

Reference

J. Conner (2017). 10 Tips to Mentor Youth like a Superstar. Retrieved from https://drjulieconnor.com/10-mentoring-tips/

10

Pray For Your Teens

Knowledge to Apply

Always pray for your teens every day for God to lead them, protect them and guide them

Reference

Omartian, S. (2014). The Power of a Praying® Parent. Harvest House Publishers.

11

Discuss Consequences with Your Teen

Knowledge to Apply

Always talk with your teen and discuss the consequences of their actions before they happen

Reference

Amber, J. (2010). Engaging, Ensuring and Elevating: Essential Strategies for Mentoring Pregnant and Parenting Teens. Retrieved from https://nationalmentoringresourcecenter.org/images/PDF/Jeannine_AmberReport_Pregnant_and_Parenting_Teens.pdf

12

Allow Others Adults to Mentor Your Teen

Knowledge to Apply

Some parents may feel threatened by another adult in their child's life. Parents need to understand the role of a mentor. Mentors are not meant to replace the parent, and it must be made clear that they are there to be a guide and a friend rather than to take on a parental or authoritative role.

Reference

Bottomley, L.(2012). Strengthening youth-parent relationships through mentoring. Michigan State University. Retrieved from: https://www.canr.msu.edu/news/strengthening_youth_parent_rel ationships_through_mentoring

13

It Is Okay To Say You Do not Know

Knowledge to Apply

As a parent of a teen, it is always good to say the truth. At times is okay to say you do not know something if you are asked by your teen. It is okay to consult others

Reference

Academic Development Institute (2008). Parent Mentor Training. Illinois Service Resource Center

14

Include the Teens in Decision Making

Knowledge to Apply

Parents play an important role in supporting teens to make wise decisions. Parents should provide information to teens about different choices, consider the pros and cons of each option, and offer emotional support.

Reference

Miller, V. and Salek, E. (2018). Supporting Healthy Decisions. Making Important Decisions Together. https://parentandteen.com/making-decisions-together/

15

Never ask or Demand your Teens to Do Anything You Would Not Do

Knowledge to Apply

Aside from being hypocritical, it places them in an unfair position of having to choose between obeying you or following their conscience. Do not preach water and take wine. The teens are too keen to observe and copy what the adults do rather than what they say.

Reference

Munroe, M., & Burrows, D. (2007). Kingdom Parenting. Destiny Image Publishers.

16

Give Them Incentives for a Good Job Done

Knowledge to apply

Once your teen has done something good, always acknowledge it and let them know you have noticed their success. Incentives can be verbal or material.

Reference

Maxwell, J. C. (2002). Leadership 101: What every leader needs to know. HarperCollins Leadership.

17

Give Them Responsibilities and Guide Them on How to Tackle Them

Knowledge to Apply

Letting you teen do chores shows responsibility. It is a great way for your teen to learn be more independent.

Reference

Morin, A. (2019). 5 Tips to Raise an Independent Teen to Become a Responsible Adult. Parenting strategies that equip kids for the real world. Retrieved from: https://www.verywellfamily.com/raising-a-teen-to-become-a-responsible-adult-4092353

18

Have Fun Together With Your Teen

Knowledge to Apply

Today's parents are busy looking for money and forget the attention of their teen. In turn their teens feel distant and may try and find comfort from other places for example drugs and bad company. Hence, the parents should find out what kind of activities your teen enjoys and do it together with them to strengthen their bond.

Reference

J. Conner (2017). 10 Tips to Mentor Youth like a Superstar. Retrieved from https://drjulieconnor.com/10-mentoring-tips/

19

Enroll Your Teen in a Mentorship Programme

Knowledge to Apply

It is the responsibility of the parent/guardian to enroll their teen in a mentoring program either at school or church so that the teens can get additional guidance.

Reference

Mentoring resource center (2015). Involving Parents in Mentoring Programs. Mentoring fact sheet. U.S. Department of Education

20

Guide Your Teen to Fulfill Their Own Dreams in Life

Knowledge to Apply

Recognize your teen's dreams and guide them through those dreams and avoid imposing your failed dreams to them. Also guide them in dreaming big.

Reference

Pearman, C. B., & Newhem, I. B. (2014). Dream So Big: A Parent's Guide to Helping Your Child Believe and Achieve. Sterling & Lord.

21

Know Your Parenting Personality

Knowledge to Apply

As a parent, be aware of how your personality and that of your teen interacts in such a way that you are both winners.

Reference

Levine, J. (2003). Know your parenting personality: How to use the enneagram to become the best parent you can be. John Wiley & Sons.

22

Let Your Teens Be Teens

Knowledge to Apply

Treat your teenagers like a teenager and not like an adult

Reference

Forward, S. (2009). Toxic parents: Overcoming their hurtful legacy and reclaiming your life. Bantam.

23

Never Ridicule, Belittle, Scorn, or Embarrass Your Teen, Especially in Public

Knowledge to Apply

Teens have a sense of pride and self-esteem which can be broken easily. Wait until you are alone with them or call them aside and communicate your feeling about something they did wrong. This may also allow give them a chance to realize their mistake.

Reference

Munroe, M., & Burrows, D. (2007). Kingdom Parenting. Destiny Image Publishers.

24

Listen To Your Teen

Knowledge to Apply

Always be ready to listen to your teenager.

Whether it make sense or not

Reference

J. Conner (2017). 10 Tips to Mentor Youth like a Superstar.
Retrieved from https://drjulieconnor.com/10-mentoring-tips/

25

When Your Teen Melts Down, Keep Your Cool

Knowledge to Apply

As a parent, try and stay calm when your teen is upset. This will help your teen to cultivate ways to calm themselves. Try and empathize with them.

Reference

Markham, L. (2012). Peaceful parent, happy kids: How to stop yelling and start connecting. TarcherPerigee.

26

Build Up Trust with Your Teen

Knowledge to Apply

This is a two way thing, not only do you have to be trusted by your teen, but you will need to trust them too. You can start off by making sure that you are at least on friendly terms with each other.

Reference

Josephson, M. S., Peter, V. J., Dowd, T., & Dowd, T. P. (2001). Parenting to Build Character in Your Teen. Boys Town Press.

27

Ask You Teen about Anything That Is Concerning You

Knowledge to Apply

If you notice any change in your teens behavior, encourage them to talk to you about it and take action by intervening where and when necessary. Let them know that you do care about them and that you will always be prepared to listen to them no matter what.

Reference

Hébert, T. P., & Neumeister, K. L. S. (2001). Guided viewing of film: A strategy for counseling gifted teenagers. Journal of Secondary Gifted Education, *12*(4), 224-235.

28

Have Faith in Your Teen

Knowledge to Apply

As a parent believe that your teen has the power to change and that it sometimes takes more than just a push but a great leap. Showing that you genuinely believe in them will help you build your relationship with your teen.

Reference

Benson, P. L. (2008). Sparks: How parents can ignite the hidden strengths of teenagers. John Wiley & Sons.

29

Have Realistic Goals and Expectations for and With Your Teen

Knowledge to apply

Set goals together with your teen. Let them be SMART (specific, measurable, attainable, realistic and time bound)

Reference

Walsh, D., & Walsh, E. (2014). Why Do They Act That Way?-Revised and Updated: A Survival Guide to the Adolescent Brain for You and Your Teen. Simon and Schuster.

30

Be a Friend to Your Teen

Knowledge to Apply

Do not just be a parent or authority figure to them. Be a friend to them

Reference

Schleifer, J. (1999). Everything you need to know about teen suicide. The Rosen Publishing Group, Inc.

31

Work as a Team

Knowledge to Apply

Parents/guardians should work together to mentor the teen and speak in one voice. That is if one parent/guardian tells the teen to stop using drugs then the other parent/guardian should not give a contrary opinion especially not in front of the teen.

Reference

Zimmerman, M. A., Bingenheimer, J. B., & Behrendt, D. E. (2005). Natural mentoring relationships. Handbook of youth mentoring, 143-157.

32

Be Godly

Knowledge to Apply

Always attend your place of worship with your teen.

Reference

Anderson, K. R., & Reese, R. D. (1999). Spiritual mentoring: A guide for seeking & giving direction. Intervarsity Press.

33

Have Family Time

Knowledge to Apply

Make time out of your busy schedule and have family time where you can take dinner, pray together with your teen.

Reference

Gibbs, N. (2006). The magic of the family meal. Time Magazine, *167*(50), 12.

34

Be Respectful to Your Teen

Knowledge to Apply

Any time you encourage your teen to share their ideas with you, without criticizing or putting them down, you show respect. Giving specific feedback also shows respect, whether you are giving praise, correction or suggestions for improvement

Reference

Apter, T. E. (2001). The myth of maturity: What teenagers need from parents to become adults? WW Norton & Company.

Be Real With Your Teen

Knowledge to Apply

Let your teen get to know you and you will seem more real to them, and not just another authority figure at home. Share stories about your own life, work place, friends, places you love etc.

Reference

Honeycutt, B. (2014). Ten Parenting Mistakes That Can Negatively Impact a Child's Future. Retrieved from: https://www.lifehack.org/articles/lifestyle/ten-parenting-mistakes-that-can-negatively-impact-childs-future.html

36

Show Empathy to Your Teen

Knowledge to Apply

When your teen is going through hard times, remember how it felt when you experienced a similar problem or loss. Try to imagine how your teen feels.

Reference

Pickhardt, C. (2018). Adolescence and the Power of Empathy. Expressing emotional awareness and caring for the teenager's feelings matters. Retrieved from https://www.psychologytoday.com/intl/blog/surviving-your-childs-adolescence/201806/adolescence-and-the-power-empathy

37

See Your Teen as an Individual

Knowledge to Apply

Identify what is special and unique about your teen and acknowledge it. Do not compare

Reference

Stuart, T. (2008). Six Ways to Build Your Teen's Identity. Retrieved from: https://www.focusonthefamily.com/parenting/six-ways-to-build-your-teens-identity/

38

Do not Criticize Your Teens Past

Knowledge to Apply

Yes, your teen might have done many mistakes in the past, Avoid bringing them up in the present.

Reference

Family lives (2017). What your teenager needs. Retrieved from: https://www.familylives.org.uk/advice/teenagers/you-and-your-teen/what-your-teenager-needs/

39

Do not Generalize Your Teen's Negative Behaviour

Knowledge to Apply

Avoid using phrases like "you always" or "you never" to your teen.

Reference

David, T. (2015). 7 Things to Stop Saying to Your Teen Immediately. What worked for your toddler won't work for your teen. Retrieved from:

https://www.psychologytoday.com/us/blog/the-magic-human-connection/201501/7-things-stop-saying-your-teen-immediately

40

Respect Your Teen's Boundaries

Knowledge to Apply

If you sense that a question you have asked your teen is a sensitive or "touchy" subject, it is good to back off and give your teen sometime.

Reference

Herndason, T. (2010). Parenting. Retrieved from: https://lifecoachingforparents.com/category/parenting/

41

Confront You Teen Thoughtfully

Knowledge to Apply

If you feel you have to convey concern or displeasure to your teen, do so in a way that also conveys reassurance and acceptance.

Reference

Power 4 youth (2019). Mentor tips. Retrieved from:

http://power4youth.org/mentor-tips/

42

Providing Academic Help and Tutoring to Your Teen

Knowledge to Apply

Teens do better in school when parents support their academic efforts. This help should be both at home with homework and at school in attending parents and open days

Reference

Hoffses, K. (2018). 10 Ways to Help Your Teen Succeed in High School. Retrieved from:

https://kidshealth.org/en/parents/school-help-teens.html

43

Provide Career Exploration Assistance to Your Teen

Knowledge to Apply

Parents play a major role in raising career aspirations for their teens. Without parental approval or support, teens are less likely to pursue diverse career possibilities. It is important for parents to learn about the many opportunities in today's schools to help students prepare for careers and postsecondary education.

Reference

Eastland-Fairfield Career & Technical Schools (2000). Parents' guide to career exploration; For middle school students. 4300 Amalgamated Place, Groveport, OH 43125/614-836-4530

44

Provide Emotional Support to Your Teen

Knowledge to Apply

Encourage your teen to talk to you. Listen and help them understand their feelings.

Reference

American Academy of Family Physicians (2018). Understanding Your Teen's Emotional Health. Retrieved from: https://familydoctor.org/understanding-your-teens-emotional-health/

45

Teach Your Teen to Be Resilient

Knowledge to Apply

Teach your child how to make it through the tough times. Help them cope with change, manage stress, and learn from setbacks.

Reference

American Academy of Family Physicians (2018). Understanding Your Teen's Emotional Health. Retrieved from: https://familydoctor.org/understanding-your-teens-emotional-health/

46

Talk With Your Teen about Sex

Knowledge to Apply

Always talk one-on-one, privately. Choose a time and place to conducive a candid conversation. Let them here it from you first and not from the media or their peers

Reference

Weeks, J. (2016). The new age of sex education: How to talk to your teen about cybersex and pornography in the digital age. Book Baby.

47

Talk With Your Teen about Drugs

Knowledge to Apply

Maintain a constant dialogue with your teen about drugs. Help your teen to be able to say the magic word "no" over and over again by teaching them delayed gratification and building their self-esteem and confidence

Reference

Partnership for Drug-Free-Kids (2018). Preventing Teen or Young Adult Drug Use: How to Talk With Your Child. Retrieved from: https://drugfree.org/article/how-to-talk-with-your-teen/

48

Reduce the Negative Impact of the Entertainment World

Knowledge to Apply

Limit the amount of time your child spends watching TV/videos. Determine a reasonable daily limit and stick to it!

Reference

KidsHealth Medical Experts (2018). How Media Use Affects Your Child. Retrieved from: https://kidshealth.org/en/parents/tv-affects-child.html

49

Understand Your Teens Character

Knowledge to Apply

Recognizing and understanding the unique differences in your teen in terms of personality differences and human behavior

Reference

Boyd, C. F. (2000). Different children, different needs: Understanding the unique personality of your child. Multnomah.

50

Allow Your Teen to Grow In Independence

Knowledge to Apply

Our job as parents is to prepare them for full independence by allowing them to grow in independence through the years.

Refcrence

Raising Children Network (2019). Independence: what does it mean for teenagers? Retrieved from:
https://raisingchildren.net.au/pre-teens/development/social-emotional-development/independence-in-teens

51

Give Your Teen House Chores

Knowledge to Apply

As parents, it is our responsibility to teach our teens the skills necessary for performing their chores. Teach them to be responsible in the house

Reference

Momentum Life (2019). 7 Important reasons why kids should have chores. Retrieved from:

https://www.momentumlife.co.nz/stories/why-kids-should-have-chores

52

When Raising Teens Learn to Say No Sometimes

Knowledge to Apply

Teens can be so demanding and it is your responsibility as a parent to weigh their demands by prioritizing them and saying no when it calls for it.

Reference

Sonenshein, S. (2017). To Raise Better Kids, Say No. retrieved from: https://www.nytimes.com/2017/05/17/well/family/to-raise-better-kids-say-no.html

53

Teach Your Teens Life Skills

Knowledge to Apply

Teach your teen life skills such as self-care and domestic living, recreation and leisure, communication and social skills, vocational skills, and other skills vital for community participation.

Reference

Abobo, F., & Orodho, J. A. (2014). Life skills education in Kenya: An assessment of the level of preparedness of teachers and school managers in implementing life skills education in Trans-Nzoia district, Kenya. IOSR Journal of Humanities and Social Science, 19(9), 32-44.

54

Encourage Your Teen to Help Out

Knowledge to Apply

Giving to the community will help your teen see that he has the power to make a difference in someone's life. It is good for his self-esteem and it will help him become a proactive adult who is invested in solving problems and supporting others.

Reference

Morin, A. (2019). 5 Tips to Raise an Independent Teen to Become a Responsible Adult. Parenting strategies that equip kids for the real world. Retrieved from:

https://www.verywellfamily.com/raising-a-teen-to-become-a-responsible-adult-4092353

55

Build Their Confidence and Self-Esteem

Knowledge to Apply

Praise them—and be specific. Tell them exactly why you are impressed or proud of them. Spend time with them, and let them know how much you value them.

Reference

American Academy of Family Physicians (2018). Understanding Your Teen's Emotional Health. Retrieved from: https://familydoctor.org/understanding-your-teens-emotional-health/

56

Provide You Teen Safety and Security

Knowledge to Apply

Give them unconditional love. Maintain routines so they feel secure. Make sure they know home is a safe place for them.

Reference

American Academy of Family Physicians (2018). Understanding Your Teen's Emotional Health. Retrieved from: https://familydoctor.org/understanding-your-teens-emotional-health/

57

Be Honest To Your Teen about Your Own Mistakes

Knowledge to Apply

As a parent instead of setting rules or giving consequences, tell them why you think they should or should not do something by sharing mistakes you have made and how you learned from them.

Reference

Garringer, M., & Jucovy, L. (2008). Building relationships: A guide for new mentors. Washington, DC: Hamilton Fish Institute on Community and School Violence.

58

As a Parent, Be Able to Push but Just Enough

Knowledge to Apply

Teens appreciate when parents push them beyond what they may have imagined they could accomplish.

Reference

Mitchell M. P. (2013). Mentoring Youth Matters. Six qualities that make you a good mentor for teens. Retrieved from: https://www.psychologytoday.com/us/blog/the-moment-youth/201301/mentoring-youth-matters

59

Improve Your Teens Social Skills

Knowledge to Apply

Make teen's better leaders by enabling them to relate to different kinds of people. Help them develop strong communication skills so they can handle any situation.

Reference

Envision (2014). 5 Ways a Mentor Can Help a Student Succeed. Retrieved from: https://www.envisionexperience.com/blog/5-ways-a-mentor-can-help-a-student-succeed

60

Motivate Your Teen

Knowledge to Apply

As a parent encourage your teen to learn, explore and have positive thinking

Reference

Awareness, C. A. (2009). High School Teen Mentoring Handbook.

Allow Your Teen to Have Voice and Choice in Deciding on Activities

Knowledge to Apply

Ask your teen what they would like to do during your time together. This ensures that they will be interested and engaged in the activity you do together.

Reference

Youth Build (2014). Tips for Being a Great Mentor. Retrieved from: http://youthbuildmentoringalliance.org/content/tips-being-great-mentor

62

Let Your Teen Control the Direction of the Conversations

Knowledge to Apply

Do not push your teen to tell you everything at once; allow them time to get to trust you. Be sensitive and respectful and above all keep everything your teen tells you confidential.

Reference

Youth Build (2014). Tips for Being a Great Mentor. Retrieved from: http://youthbuildmentoringalliance.org/content/tips-being-great-mentor

63

If Possible, Monitor What Your Teen Watches Online

Knowledge to Apply

Use internet filters to prevent your teens from going to unwanted sites. Teens spend a lot of time online, surfing the web, playing violent games, watching pornography, chatting or shop online. Internet use has been shown to causes social isolation, depression and in extreme cases suicide.

Reference

Gross, E. F. (2004). Adolescent Internet use: What we expect, what teens report. Journal of applied developmental psychology, 25(6), 633-649.

64

Teens Also Undergo Stress: Help Them Manage It

Knowledge to Apply

Do not put too much pressure on your teen. Research shows that the most frequently noted stressor among teens was school (maintaining good grades), followed by money, relationships (sex, STD/AIDS, becoming pregnant) and parents.

Reference

LaRue, D. E., & Herrman, J. W. (2008). Adolescent stress through the eyes of high-risk teens. Pediatric nursing, 34(5).

65

Give Your Teen Time to Relax and Unwind

Knowledge to Apply

Just like parents, teens need time to do something they enjoy each day. Be it sports, reading a book or playing on the computer, allow them a few minutes of personal time. Where possible monitor and let it be time-bound

Reference

Vivo, M. (2010). 10 Things Teens Wish Their Parents Knew. Retrieved from: https://aspeneducation.crchealth.com/10-things-teens-wish-their-parents-knew/

66

As Parents, Never Fight in Front of Your Teens

Knowledge to Apply

Always settle your differences in private. Teens watch their parents carefully to understand how relationships work. They need strong role models who show them how to treat others with respect even if they do not always agree. Conflict at home is unsettling for everyone in the house.

Reference

Vivo, M. (2010). 10 Things Teens Wish Their Parents Knew. Retrieved from: https://aspeneducation.crchealth.com/10-things-teens-wish-their-parents-knew/

Meet Their Friends

Knowledge to Apply

Give everyone your teen shows interest in a chance. This does not mean you have to like them, but you should at least take the relationship as serious as your teen wants to. If the boyfriend or girlfriend is not treating your teen right you need to draw a line. They might be mad at you for it, but at least you gave them a chance.

Reference

Nelson, C. (2016). 10 Things Teenagers Need To Hear From Their Parents. The teenage years are usually the hardest, for both the teenager and the parents. Retrieved from: https://www.theodysseyonline.com/10-things-teenagers-need-to-hear-from-their-parents

68

Do Not Speak To Your Teens As If They Are Little Kids

Knowledge to Apply

Parenting styles must change if you wish to keep your relationships with your teen strong. This includes not only the content but also the tone of conversation. You need to treat them more like adults than children. Truly listen and heed their point of view, even if you disagree with them.

Reference

Duffy, J. (2011). The Available Parent: Radical Optimism for Raising Teens and Tweens. Cleis Press.

69

As A Parent, Educate Yourself

Knowledge to Apply

As a parent, read books about teenagers. Think back on your own teen years. Remember your struggles you went through at your development years. Expect some mood changes from your typically sunny child, and be prepared for more conflict as he or she matures as an individual. Parents who know what is coming can cope with it better. And the more you know, the better you can prepare.

Reference

KidsHealth Medical Experts (2019). A Parent's Guide to Surviving the Teen Years. Retrieved from:
https://kidshealth.org/en/parents/adolescence.html.

70

Pick Which Battles to Fight with Your Teen

Knowledge to Apply

If you teen want to dye their hair, paint their fingernails black, or wear funky clothes, think twice before you object. Teens want to shock their parents and it is a lot better to let them do something temporary and harmless; save your battles for things that really matter, like alcohol and substance abuse, or permanent changes to their appearance.

Reference

Kids Health Medical Experts (2019). A Parent's Guide to Surviving the Teen Years. Retrieved from:
https://kidshealth.org/en/parents/adolescence.html.

71

Know the Warning Signs So That You Can Intervene

Knowledge to Apply

A certain amount of change is normal during the teen years. But too drastic or long-lasting switch in personality or behavior may be a sign of real trouble that needs your intervention. Example, extreme weight gain or loss, falling grades, criminal activity etc.

Reference

KidsHealth Medical Experts (2019). A Parent's Guide to Surviving the Teen Years. Retrieved from:
https://kidshealth.org/en/parents/adolescence.html.

72

Inspect Your Teen's Devices

Knowledge to Apply

See who and what they are texting. Look at their social media accounts. Check out the types of apps and games they are downloading. Ignorance of technology is not an excuse. Your child's media consumption is shaping their identity. As a parent, you have an obligation to monitor, filter, and even control it.

Reference

Linder A. (2018). 5 Things Every Parent of Teens Need to Do More Often. Retrieved from: https://www.allprodad.com/5-things-every-parent-of-teens-need-to-do-more-often/

73

Attend Your Teen's School Events

Knowledge to Apply

Your schedule may prevent you from going to every school event, but make an effort to be there for the most important ones. This will show your teen that you interested in their school life

Reference

LifeCare (2011). Positive Parenting Strategies for the Teenage Years.

https://www.wfm.noaa.gov/pdfs/ParentingYourTeen_Handout1.pdf

74

Never do Work for Your Teen

Knowledge to Apply

If you do your teens work, be it school work or house chores, the lesson you are teaching your teen is that he or she can avoid responsibility.

Reference

Life Care (2011). Positive Parenting Strategies for the Teenage Years.
https://www.wfm.noaa.gov/pdfs/ParentingYourTeen_Handout1.pdf

75

Discuss Poor Grades with Your Teen and Come Up with a Plan for Improvement

Knowledge to Apply

Ask your teen why they felt they received the poor grade and brainstorm ideas on how they can improve. By talking to your teen, you can help them recognize that their academic performance is a direct reflection of their work and study habits—and consequently, they have the power to change it.

Reference

LifeCare (2011). Positive Parenting Strategies for the Teenage Years. https://www.wfm.noaa.gov/pdfs/ParentingYourTeen_Handout1.pdf

76

Encourage Your Teen to Read

Knowledge to Apply

Make books, magazines and newspapers available in your home. Be a role model by reading often. You may even want to choose books with your teen that you will both read and discuss later.

Reference

LifeCare (2011). Positive Parenting Strategies for the Teenage Years.
https://www.wfm.noaa.gov/pdfs/ParentingYourTeen_Handout1.pdf

77

Do Not Give in to Requests for Extra Money

Knowledge to Apply

Once you have agreed on an amount (pocket money etc.) with your teen, try not to give in to requests for more money. Strict adherence is the only way your teen truly learns how to manage their money.

Reference

LifeCare (2011). Positive Parenting Strategies for the Teenage Years.
https://www.wfm.noaa.gov/pdfs/ParentingYourTeen_Handout1.pdf

Do Not Push Your Teen into Independence Before they are Ready

Knowledge to Apply

Every teen has his own timetable for blossoming into an independent person. It is NOT healthy for your child to feel that you are pushing him into independence - that only leads to him becoming overly dependent on the peer group for validation.

Reference

Markham, L (2019). Game plan for Positive Parenting Your Teen. Retrieved from: https://www.ahaparenting.com/Ages-stages/teenagers/parenting-teens

Stay Connected to Your Teen as They Move Into the World

Knowledge to Apply

If we have accepted our teen's dependency needs and affirmed her development into her own separate person, she will stay fiercely connected to us even as her focus shifts to peers, high school and the passions that make her soul sing. Teens who are well grounded in their families will respond well to parents' efforts to stay connected.

Reference

Markham, L (2019). Game plan for Positive Parenting Your Teen. Retrieved from: https://www.ahaparenting.com/Ages-stages/teenagers/parenting-teens

80

Encourage Your Teen to Sleep

Knowledge to Apply

As a parent make sure that your teen has enough sleep by controlling television hours. Your teen's bedroom should be quiet and dark. Avoid heavy meals, sugars and caffeine at night and having a routine time of going to bed and waking up.

Reference

Hayes, L. (2018). 14 tips for parents with teenagers from teen expert Louise Hayes. Retrieved from: https://www.inspiro.org.au/blog/14-parenting-tips-for-teens

81

Remind Your Teens to Ask For Help

Knowledge to Apply

Let your teen know that they do not have to make choices alone. Ensure that they save contacts of people (siblings, parents, or extended family) who can be available to talk through options if they are in a difficult situation

Reference

McCue, J. (2018). A parent's guide to why teens make bad decisions. Retrieved from: http://theconversation.com/a-parents-guide-to-why-teens-make-bad-decisions-88246

82

Use Mistakes as Learning Opportunities

Knowledge to Apply

Teenagers may make some wrong choices. Use these lived experiences to generate discussion about where the decision making went wrong, and how to make better choices in the future.

Reference

McCue, J. (2018). A parent's guide to why teens make bad decisions. Retrieved from: http://theconversation.com/a-parents-guide-to-why-teens-make-bad-decisions-88246

83

Ignore Mild Forms of Disrespect

Knowledge to Apply

It is usually best to ignore mildly disrespectful behaviour such as shrugging the shoulders, raised eyebrows, feigned boredom, or muttering under the breath. Disrespectful behaviour in teenagers is common and is part of the process of growing up. But blatant rudeness should never be tolerated. Ignoring it will simply lead to an escalation of such behaviour.

Reference

Wong, D. (2018). How to Deal With a Disrespectful Teenager: 10 Tips for Frustrated Parents. Retrieved from: https://www.daniel-wong.com/2018/03/19/disrespectful-teenager/

84

The Right or Wrong Crowd for Your Teen

Knowledge to Apply

Friends can be a tricky subject for both teens and parents. Parents want their children to hang out with the right kind of crowd. But teens want to be able to make their own friend choices. While hanging out with the wrong crowd can be worrisome, parents need to focus on their teen's behavior rather than the behavior of their friends. Set clear boundaries and have a faith that your teen will make the right choices. Help your teen navigate through friendships that might be toxic to them in a calm loving manner.

Reference

Betts, J. L (2006). Common Problems between Parents and Teenagers. Retrieved from:

https://teens.lovetoknow.com/Parent_Teenager_Problems

85

Stay Calm and Discuss

Knowledge to Apply

The best way to handle any unexpected situation with teens is to stay calm, listen and discuss the issue with them. Overreacting with anger or displeasure will not get you any positive results. The best approach is to have an open discussion with your teen.

Reference

Secure teen (2013). Should Parents Allow Their Teens To Have Tattoos? Retrieved from: https://www.secureteen.com/values-traditions/should-parents-allow-their-teens-to-have-tattoos/

86

Practice Social Parenting

Knowledge to Apply

As a parent you may not be very knowledgeable with social media, but new research shows that you should not shy away from sending your teen a friend request on Facebook or engaging them on Twitter, Instagram and other social platforms. Teens feel closer to parents when they connect online.

Reference

Brigham Young University (2013). Social parenting: Teens feel closer to parents when they connect online. Retrieved from: https://phys.org/news/2013-07-social-parenting-teens-closer-parents.html

87

Get Outside Information about Your Teen

Knowledge to Apply

Find out from other people who know your teen (coaches, teachers, friends and parents of friends) whether your teen seems different around them. Teens might feel ashamed and may not want to burden their family, so they may reveal more to someone else they trust than to their parents.

Reference

Nierenberg, C (2016). 8 Tips for Parents of Teens with Depression. Retrieved from: https://www.livescience.com/56601-teens-depression-signs-tips-parents.html

88

Your Approval or Disapproval Teaches Your Child about Desirable Behavior

Knowledge to Apply

As a Parent you need to be careful about how you express your approval or disapproval. Parents who are harsh in their disapproval may hurt their children's self-esteem; parents who never express disapproval may raise children who cannot deal with any criticism. Try to find a balance between expressions of approval and disapproval. Be consistent in your rewards and punishments.

Reference

Grace point (2019). Mentoring. Retrieved from:

https://www.gracepointwellness.org/82-parenting/article/4732-mentoring

89

Let Your Mentorship be All Round

Knowledge to Apply

In the past parents were most concerned about character and right and wrong. Today our greater concern is with academic achievement, a stance that accepts a generally characterless educational system. Let us mentor our teens in both the academic and behavior area

Reference

Gauld, J. W. (2014). Parents: Start Mentoring Your Kids! Retrieved from: https://www.huffpost.com/entry/start-mentoring-your-kids_b_4025353

90

Challenge Your Teen

Knowledge to Apply

If you discover your teen is wrestling with a particular issue, challenge them to grow in those areas. It is best to start with small wins, which will motivate progress towards a larger goal. As small victories increase, challenge them with bigger things.

Reference

Johnson, S. (2014). A Guide on How to Mentor Youth in the Church. Retrieved from: https://www.faithventures.com/a-guide-on-how-to-mentor-youth/

Do Follow-Ups with Your Teen

Knowledge to Apply

As a parent, hold your teen accountable to the goals they have set. Without follow-ups their growth will stunt and their progress will stall. Without check-ins, teens may feel as if your connection is fading, and that is the last thing we want! Youths crave for someone to come alongside them, to teach them, and to guide them.

Reference

Johnson, S. (2014). A Guide on How to Mentor Youth in the Church. Retrieved from: https://www.faithventures.com/a-guide-on-how-to-mentor-youth/

92

Fathers Should Actively Participate in Mentoring their Teens

Knowledge to Apply

No matter how busy you are as a father, be ready to mentor your teen. A recent study showed that 51% of teens receive mentorship from their mothers compared to 5% who received mentorship from their fathers. There is a strong positive relationship between adolescents having an adult mentor and decreased participation in risky behaviors.

Reference

Beier S. R, Rosenfeld W. D, Spitalny K. C, Zansky S. M, Bontempo A. N. (2000). The Potential Role of an Adult Mentor in Influencing High-Risk Behaviors in Adolescents. Arch Pediatr Adolesc Med. 2000;154(4):327–331.

93

Use Reflective Statements When Mentoring Teens

Knowledge to Apply

As a parent always repeat back what your teen has said to summarize their situation, thoughts, or feelings. Reflective statements give both you and your teen an opportunity to ensure that you understand one another and your teen knows that you were listening.

Reference

Girls' Success (2009). Mentoring Guide for Life Skills. AED Center for Gender Equity. Retrieved from:
http://www.ungei.org/resources/files/LifeSkills.pdf

94

Probe Your Teen Gently Instead of Demanding

Knowledge to Apply

Your approach to dealing with your troubled teenager should change as you see your child improve in his conduct. You should deal with him firmly and gently instead of an unconditionally strict approach. When you are inquiring about anything, be gentle and friendly.

Reference

Tun, R. (2017). 10 Steps On How To Mentor Troubled Teens. Retrieved from: https://smiletutor.sg/10-steps-on-how-to-mentor-troubled-teens/

95

Be Mindful of Your Facial Expression and Body Posture

Knowledge to Apply

If as a parent you seem distracted or uncomfortable when you are mentoring your teen, they will notice and negative feelings or thoughts will cause them to think that you do not really want to be there for them.

Reference

Wikihow (2017). How to Mentor Teens. Retrieved from:
https://www.wikihow.com/Mentor-Teens

96

Be Able to Identify the Root Cause

Knowledge to Apply

As a parent, some issues will be easy for you to relate to and offer good positive advice like how to choose a good career or relationship problems, etc. However, there might be something far worse happening in your teen's life. These are issues like abuse, drug/alcohol addiction, suicide thoughts etc.

Reference

Wikihow (2017). How to Mentor Teens. Retrieved from:
https://www.wikihow.com/Mentor-Teens

97

Ask Your Teen Open-Ended Questions

Knowledge to Apply

As a parent with a teen, open-ended questions allow for clarification and a deeper exploration of a topic. Asking questions starting with who, what, where, how or why invites more of a response versus questions that only require a 'yes' or 'no' answer

Reference

Ambassador Girls' Scholarship Program (2008). Girls' Mentoring Resource Guide. USAID, Retrieved from: https://www.worlded.org/WEIInternet/inc/common/download pub.cfm?id=10295&lid=3

98

As a Parent, do Not Expect Perfection

Knowledge to Apply

Parenting is an art, not a science. Successful parents understand that, like themselves, their teens are not perfect either. This frees them to love their children unreservedly.

Reference

All pro dad (2018). 7 Characteristics of Successful Parents. Retrieved from: https://www.allprodad.com/7-characteristics-of-successful-parents/

Have a Sense of Humor

Knowledge to Apply

Parents with a healthy sense of humor are the most popular with teens. Good humor encourages open and unrestrained dialogue in families and provides relief from life's stressors. It also reduces stress hormones, stimulates endorphins, and strengthens the immune system. Most importantly, it makes family time more fun.

Reference

Grover, S. (2015). 10 Characteristics in the most outstanding parents. Retrieved from:
http://www.themomiverse.com/motherhood-and-family/10-best-parenting-qualities/

100

Show your Teens You Love Them Every Day

Knowledge to Apply

As parents we can all get so busy, it is easy to forget to take the time to show our teens how we feel about them. Small gestures, like writing a little note for them on the fridge or sharing things about yourself with them can strengthen your connection and show your teen how much you love them every day.

Reference

Lee, K. (2019). What Are Traits of Good Parents? Retrieved from: https://www.verywellfamily.com/things-that-good-parents-do-620051

101

Be Patient with Your Teen

Knowledge to Apply

It is true: Good things come to those who wait. Be patient with your teen. "Let us not become weary in doing good, for at the proper time we will reap a harvest if we do not give up". (Galatians 6:9)

Reference

Holy Bible, New International Version®, NIV® Copyright ©1973, 1978, 1984, 2011 by Biblica, Inc.® .

About the authors

Dr Felicity W. Githinji holds a Doctor of Philosophy (Ph D) in Sociology of Education, a Master of Education in Sociology of Education, a Bachelor of Education (Special Education/Home-economics) from Kenyatta University and a Post-Doctoral from The Council for the Development of Social Science Research in Africa (CODESRIA) and has a wide knowledge and experience in Mentoring and Academic Advising in all levels of academic advancements and family life. She has experience in teaching teens from primary, secondary school and at university level. She is currently a full-time Senior lecturer in Moi University.

Gerald G. Githinji holds a Master of Science in plant breeding and biotechnology (University of Eldoret), a Post Graduate Diploma in Education (biology and chemistry options) (Moi University) and a Bachelor of Science Degree (biochemistry) (Kenyatta University). He has experience in teaching teens at secondary school level and university level. He is a sessional assistant lecturer at Technical University of Kenya and currently working with the Ministry of Health as a chief biochemist.

Mary W. Muhia holds a Bachelor of Education (Arts – Kiswahili/CRE options) (University of Nairobi). She has been teaching in several high schools and has experience in mentoring teens. She has also enrolled for a Master's degree course.